JUST BE YOU

summersdale

JUST BE YOU

Compiled by Peggy Jones

An Hachette UK Company
www.hachette.co.uk

Summersdale Publishers Ltd
Part of Octopus Publishing Group Limited
Carmelite House
50 Victoria Embankment
LONDON
EC4Y 0DZ
UK

www.summersdale.com

Printed and bound in China

ISBN: 978-1-80007-184-1

Substantial discounts on bulk quantities of Summersdale books are available to corporations, professional associations and other organizations. For details contact general enquiries: telephone: +44 (0) 1243 771107 or email: enquiries@summersdale.com.

To..

From..

Dare to love yourself as if you were a rainbow with gold at both ends.

Aberjhani

You don't
have to be
perfect to be
wonderful

I am my
own experiment.
I am my own
work of art.

Madonna

LOOK INSIDE YOURSELF AND FIND YOUR OWN INNER STRENGTH.

Mariah Carey

NOT PERFECT
– NOT TRYING
TO BE

You decide what you are, what you want to express.

Gianni Versace

Be available for life to happen.

Bill Murray

You're only
confined by
the walls
you build
yourself

Existence wants you to be just as you are.

Osho

Being comfortable
in your own skin
is one of the most
important things
to achieve.

Kate Mara

Don't just be good to others – be good to yourself too

Put yourself first. Self-love is not selfish at all.

Laurie Hernandez

You don't
have to wait to
be confident.
Just do it
and eventually
the confidence
will follow.

Carrie Fisher

BUILT
DIFFERENT

Our uniqueness, our individuality, and our life experience moulds us into fascinating beings.

Linda Thompson

This life
is mine alone.
So I have stopped
asking people
for directions to
places they've
never been.

Glennon Doyle

ORIGINALS
ARE ALWAYS
MORE
VALUABLE
THAN COPIES

If we stop defining
each other by what
we are not and
start defining
ourselves by what
we are, we can
all be freer.

Emma Watson

Some people say you are going the wrong way, when it's simply a way of your own.

Angelina Jolie

If your heart
isn't in it,
take yourself
out of it

Never apologize for showing feeling. When you do so, you apologize for the truth.

Benjamin Disraeli

I TO MYSELF AM DEARER THAN A FRIEND.

William Shakespeare

FEELIN'
MYSELF

You're always
with yourself,
so you might
as well enjoy
the company.

Diane von Fürstenberg

**Be bold,
be brave
enough to be
your true self.**

Queen Latifah

Wonderful things happen when you realize that you're enough

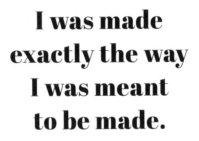

I was made exactly the way I was meant to be made.

Megan Rapinoe

Always be yourself,
express yourself,
have faith in
yourself – do not
go out and look
for a successful
personality and
duplicate it.

Bruce Lee

No one needs to like you except you

Until you value yourself, you won't value your time. Until you value your time, you will not do anything with it.

M. Scott Peck

Your self-worth
is determined by
you. You don't
have to depend on
someone telling
you who you are.

Beyoncé

I'M A GOOD
THING JUST
HOW I AM

If they don't like you for being yourself, be yourself even more.

Taylor Swift

Never be bullied into silence. Never allow yourself to be made a victim. Accept no one's definition of your life, but define yourself.

Harvey Fierstein

ACCEPT
YOURSELF
FOR ALL
THAT
YOU ARE

The inward journey
is about finding
your own fullness,
something that
no one else can
take away.

Deepak Chopra

I'm centred
in who I am, and
I'm really grateful.
I'm not perfect.

Letitia Wright

I am enough
I am talented
I am strong

I always feel
confident. I never
allow myself to not
feel confident.

Amber Rose

LOVE FLOWERS BEST IN OPENNESS AND FREEDOM.

Edward Abbey

LEARN TO
LET GO
OF WHAT
YOU CAN'T
CHANGE

The world just wants your authentic truth.

Gabby Bernstein

**All you need
is the plan,
the road map,
and the courage
to press on to
your destination.**

Earl Nightingale

Want to know
who's going
to change
your life?
Take a look
in the mirror

The fact that I'm me and no one else is one of my greatest assets.

Haruki Murakami

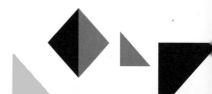

If you can't love yourself, how in the hell you gonna love somebody else?

RuPaul

There's no such thing as fear if you're true to yourself

If you're stubborn and you don't give up and you work really hard – no one else can ever be you.

P!nk

I like me.
I like my story
and all the bumps
and bruises.
I think that's
what makes me
uniquely me.

Michelle Obama

NEVER
FORGET
HOW RARE
YOU ARE

Extraordinary things are always hiding in places people never think to look.

Jodi Picoult

Find out who you are and do it on purpose.

Dolly Parton

SPEAK
LOVE TO
YOURSELF

Do not fear
to be eccentric
in opinion, for
every opinion
now accepted was
once eccentric.

Bertrand Russell

As soon as you trust yourself, you will know how to live.

Johann Wolfgang von Goethe

Don't shrink yourself to fit in

Choose to be in touch with what is wonderful, refreshing and healing within yourself and around you.

Thích Nhất Hạnh

YOU GET ONE LIFE. WHO CARES WHAT EVERYONE ELSE THINKS?

Kelly Clarkson

YOU ARE A
MASTERPIECE
AND A WORK
IN PROGRESS

Either appear as you are, or be as you appear.

Rumi

If we treated ourselves as well as we treated our best friend, can you imagine?

Meghan, Duchess of Sussex

Put yourself
at the top of
your to-do list

Have the courage to stand and say, "This is who I am."

Oprah Winfrey

In order to be
who you are, you
must be willing to
let go of who you
think you are.

Michael Singer

You just need to be real – not perfect

You can't live your
life trying to be
somebody else.
What's the point?

Lizzo

Our physical,
emotional and
spiritual health
requires rest.
We need to take
a break.

Dana Arcuri

FALL IN LOVE WITH YOURSELF

Sometimes the most important thing in a whole day is the rest we take between two deep breaths.

Etty Hillesum

With confidence, you have won even before you have started.

Marcus Garvey

SOMETIMES BEING PRODUCTIVE JUST MEANS RELAXING

There is power
in vulnerability,
connection in
empathy and
strength in
honesty.

Prince Harry, Duke of Sussex

Reassure yourself of your beauty and your affection. Make sure that you are in tune with your soul.

Debbie Allen

Self-love isn't an expense – it's an investment

When you take care
of yourself, you're
a better person for
others. When you
feel good about
yourself, you treat
others better.

Solange

ABOUT ALL YOU CAN DO IN LIFE IS BE WHO YOU ARE.

Rita Mae Brown

FORGIVE YOURSELF

I am standing for myself, within myself. I am standing for a new vision.

Iyanla Vanzant

You can't say yes to everything and not say yes to taking care of yourself.

Shonda Rhimes

Make sure
a "yes" to
someone else
isn't a "no"
to yourself

We elicit from
the world what
we project into
the world.

Bruce Perry

Don't dilute yourself
for any person or
any reason. You
are enough! Be
unapologetically you.

Steve Maraboli

Self-care isn't selfish

Believe in your heart what you know to be true about yourself.

Mary J. Blige

If you're presenting
yourself with
confidence, you can
pull off pretty
much anything.

Katy Perry

YOU'VE GOT
TO NOURISH
TO FLOURISH

The wise treat self-respect as non-negotiable.

Thomas Szasz

You can't base your life on other people's expectations.

Stevie Wonder

UNPLUG AND REBOOT

I have a confidence
about my life
that comes from
standing tall on
my own two feet.

Jane Fonda

Being perfect is being flawed, accepting it and never letting it make you feel less than your best.

Jessica Alba

Dress yourself in confidence each and every morning

Look in the mirror
and say, "You are
beautiful" and
"You are worthy."

Demi Lovato

DO YOUR THING AND DON'T CARE IF THEY LIKE IT.

Tina Fey

LET YOUR
GLOW LIGHT
THE WAY

Live in the moment, enjoy the day, make the most of what you have.

Michael J. Fox

Not one ounce of my self-worth depends on your acceptance of me.

Quincy Jones

Everything
you need –
your courage,
strength,
compassion
and love –
is already
within you

When you're in your lane, there's no traffic.

Ava DuVernay

Cherish forever
what makes you
unique, 'cuz you're
really a yawn
if it goes.

Bette Midler

Never stop growing

For me, success is inner peace.

Denzel Washington

Love yourself first
and everything else
falls into line.

Lucille Ball

PAY THEM
NO HEED

When someone is properly grounded in life, they shouldn't have to look outside themselves for approval.

Epictetus

I fall in love
with someone
because of their
flaws. And I've
learned to love
myself because
of my flaws, too.

Cara Delevingne

I AM
POWERFUL

Once you realize
that you can do
something, it would
be difficult to live
with yourself if
you didn't do it.

James Baldwin

Low self-esteem is like driving through life with your hand-brake on.

Maxwell Maltz

Authenticity over all else

Love is the greatest force in the universe. It is the heartbeat of the moral cosmos.

Martin Luther King Jr

BE YOURSELF. THE WORLD WORSHIPS THE ORIGINAL.

Ingrid Bergman

GO OUT AND
DISCOVER
WHAT
YOU'RE
CAPABLE OF

Fear kills your ability to see beauty. You have to get beyond fear, back to a comfortable space before you can even start looking around.

Will Smith

Nothing can dim the light which shines from within.

Maya Angelou

You are at your most powerful when you don't seek the approval of others

To love oneself is the beginning of a lifelong romance.

Oscar Wilde

I just want to be
happy. If that's
me just being
myself, then I
don't really care.

Selena Gomez

Comparison is the enemy of contentment

The willingness to accept responsibility for one's own life is the source from which self-respect springs.

Joan Didion

Keep chasing those moments where you discover something new about your voice. Don't ever let that end.

Octavia Spencer

LET IT GO
AND LET
YOURSELF IN

If you want to be respected by others the great thing is to respect yourself.

Fyodor Dostoevsky

No one can make you feel inferior without your consent.

Eleanor Roosevelt

CHECK
IN ON
YOURSELF

I will not let anyone walk through my mind with their dirty feet.

Mahatma Gandhi

Beauty is how you feel inside, and it reflects in your eyes. It is not something physical.

Sophia Loren

Keep that head up

The path to your
success is not
as fixed and
inflexible as
you think.

Misty Copeland

THERE IS A SELF-LOVE SOLUTION FOR EVERY CHALLENGE.

Abiola Abrams

BE A LITTLE SELFISH SOMETIMES

Be who you are and say what you feel.

Bernard M. Baruch

Never violate the sacredness of your individual self-respect.

Theodore Parker

Treat yourself
with kindness
and your soul
will smile back

You are the hero of your own story.

Joseph Campbell

Do not allow people to dim your shine because they are blinded. Tell them to put on some sunglasses!

Lady Gaga

Happiness looks great on you

Owning your story is the bravest thing you will ever do.

Brené Brown

I think in life
you should work
on yourself until
the day you die.

Serena Williams

KNOW YOUR WORTH, THEN ADD TAX

Always be a first-rate version of yourself, instead of a second-rate version of somebody else.

Judy Garland

You have to be able to love yourself because that's when things fall into place.

Vanessa Hudgens

YOU HAVE NOTHING TO PROVE TO ANYBODY

I have insecurities
of course, but I
don't hang out with
anyone who points
them out to me.

Adele

Nobody is perfect. I just don't believe in perfection.

Kate Winslet

Become
incomparable

It's okay to not be perfect, to not get it all done… Take care of yourself. Do what recharges you.

Leah Remini

BE IN LOVE WITH YOUR LIFE. EVERY MINUTE OF IT.

Jack Kerouac

EACH AND
EVERY DAY
YOU GROW A
LITTLE MORE

Don't ever let anyone stifle who you are and how you express yourself.

Ariel Winter

You protect your being when you love yourself better. That's the secret.

Isabelle Adjani

Life was created for you – live it exactly as you please

Nothing can bring you peace but yourself.

Ralph Waldo Emerson

When you can and as you can, in ways that feel loving, make time and space for yourself.

Tracee Ellis Ross

You change the world by being yourself.

Yoko Ono

JUST
BE YOU

Have you enjoyed this book?
If so, find us on Facebook at
Summersdale Publishers, on Twitter
at **@Summersdale** and on Instagram
at **@summersdalebooks** and get in
touch. We'd love to hear from you!

www.summersdale.com